D1823981

Handwriting Age 6–7

Rhona Whiteford

Rhona Whiteford has many years' experience of teaching at preschool and primary school level, and is the author of a wide range of educational books for teachers, parents and children. She has two children.

Consultant: **Andrew Burrell**

Andrew Burrell has worked as a primary school teacher and as a lecturer at the Institute of Education, University of London, and has carried out research into the teaching of Language and Literacy.

Illustrated by **Kate Sheppard**

About this book

This book contains handwriting activities suitable for 6- and 7-year-olds. They are based on the National Curriculum and National Literacy Strategy requirements for Year 2.

The activities gradually become more demanding, so it is important to start at the beginning.

The handwriting skills taught or practised in each unit are stated at the top of the page. A note at the foot of the page tells you more about the purpose of the activities and gives advice about how to help your child with them.

'Superstar' stickers are included to help motivate children. There is a space for your child to stick a star when he or she has completed a unit. The 'Look what I have learned' page at the back of the book has space for another star, and is intended to give your child a sense of achievement, while providing you with a useful checklist of skills.

Each unit ends with a positive comment. Encouragement from you will work wonders, so be generous with your praise!

How to help your child

- Find a quiet place to work, preferably sitting at a table. Good posture helps the hand and arm to move freely.

- Work with your child little and often, but don't insist if he or she is tired or happily doing something else. Help with reading the instructions where necessary.

- Make sure your child has a sharp pencil. Ballpoint pens and fountain pens are too difficult to control at this stage.

- The pencil or pen should be held between the thumb and forefinger and supported by the middle finger.

- If your child is left-handed, turn the book slightly so that he or she can see the writing as it is formed.

- Encourage your child to check his or her work.

- Give opportunities for writing notes and lists in everyday life.

Above all, be relaxed – and have fun!

Hodder Children's Books
a division of
Hachette Children's Books

The alphabet

**Look at the picture.
Practise writing the letter,
and then complete the word.**

My name is Otis, and I'm going to help you with your handwriting.

a b c d e f g h i j k l m n o p q r s t u v w x y z

a   a**rrow**   b   b**us**   c   c**at**

d   d**oor**   e   e**gg**   f   f**inger**

g   g**irl**   h   h**ouse**   i   i**nsect**

Your child will be familiar with all the unjoined lower case letters by the time he begins this book. Encourage him to trace over each letter, write it independently and then trace over the first letter of the word.

Curly f and curly k are introduced here, in preparation for joined writing which is taught later in the book. Give your child extra practice in writing them if necessary. The f has two pencil strokes, but the k should be completed in a single, fluid movement.

j	jam	k	kite	l	love
m	man	n	night	o	octopus
p	pen	q	quilt	r	ring	s	sun
t	tree	u	up	v	van
w	wag	x	six	y	yo-yo	z	zebra

The words *cat, door, girl, house, love, man, night, tree* and *up* are school words – words that your child will probably be learning by sight at school. Handwriting and spelling are both mastered most effectively if they are taught in parallel.

How did you get on with f and k?

Brilliant!

3

Capital letters

The letters on this page are made from straight lines.

Practise writing these capital letters.

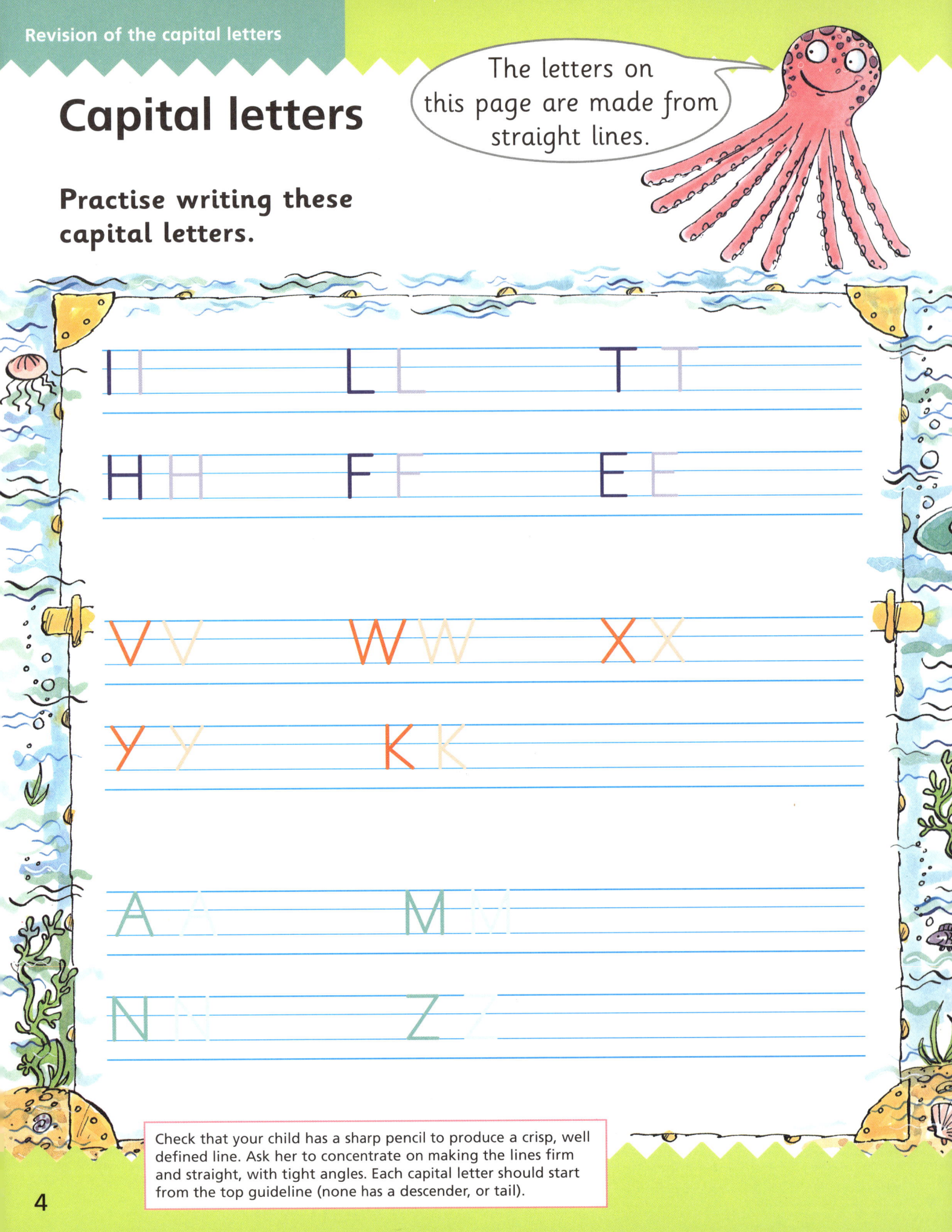

I I   L L   T T

H H   F F   E E

V V   W W   X X

Y Y   K K

A A   M M

N N   Z Z

Check that your child has a sharp pencil to produce a crisp, well defined line. Ask her to concentrate on making the lines firm and straight, with tight angles. Each capital letter should start from the top guideline (none has a descender, or tail).

**Practise writing these capital letters.
Copy the words, too.**

The letters on this page are made from curved and straight lines.

C

O

Q

CLEVER CRAB

G

S

SLIPPERY

U

J

OH, OTIS

P

R

B

D

Fantastic!

Letter sets; Join 1

Joined writing is quicker and neater!

These are the letter sets.

Set 1

a c d e h
i k l m n
s t u

Set 2

a c d e g i
j m n o p
q r s u v
w x y

Set 3

b f h
k l t

Set 4

f o r
v w

Join 1

can join

any letter in **Set 1**

to

any letter in **Set 2**

ac

Practise Join 1.

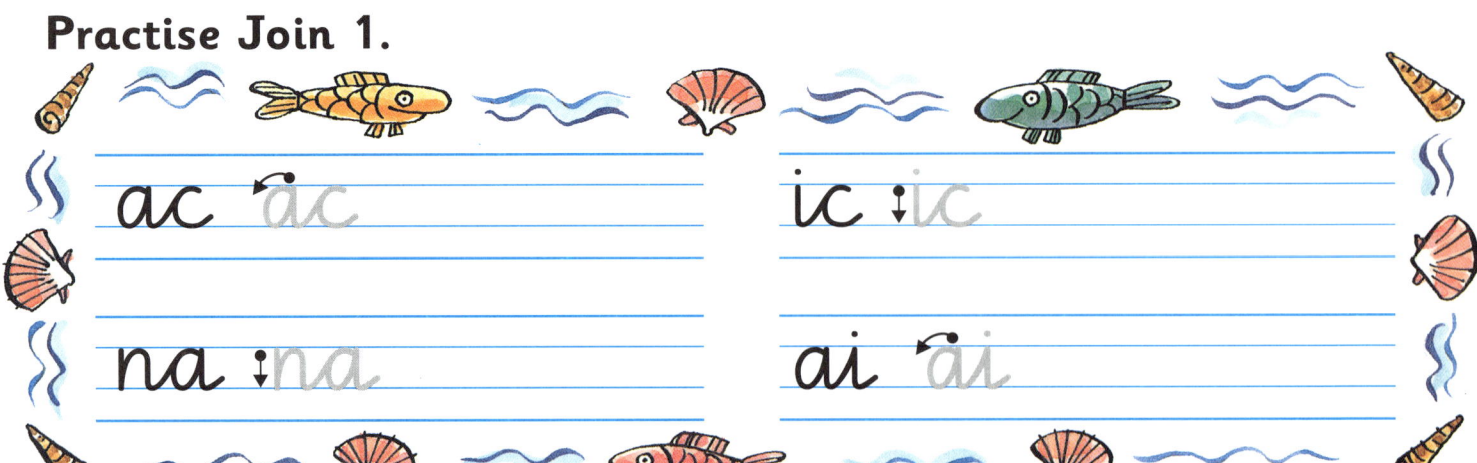

ac ac   ic ic

na na   ai ai

Most children enjoy making the transition to joined writing, appreciating the extra speed and fluency.

Letter sets: The letters are arranged in sets, according to which joins are needed to link them.

Joins: There are four kinds of join, taught in order of difficulty in this book.

More practice!

en en   un un

in in   ni ni

cr cr   tr tr

la la   da da

tu tu   kn kn

hi hi   ap ap

Take care when you are are joining **to** or **from** s!

es es

so so

Encourage your child to complete each pair of letters in a single, rhythmic movement, without lifting his pencil from the paper.

Practise Join 1 in these funny phrases.

lacy ladies up a ladder

ten tiny tummies in a tin

JELLY BABIES

many mean men in a mess

Write my name in joined writing!

Otis

Children love alliteration, and copying these humorous phrases will help to develop handwriting and spelling, as well as concentration on a task. All the phrases contain only the first join.

Make up more phrases like these with your child.

Make a list of the dressing up clothes.

I'm dressed up as an alien!

cap

canes

ties

mac

mad hair

Well written!

Join 2

Join 2
can join

Set 1
a c d e h
i k l m n
s t u

to

Set 3
b f h
k l t

at

any letter in **Set 1**

any letter in **Set 3**

Practise Join 2.

et   *et*   ab   *ab*

ch   *ch*   ck   *ck*

al   *al*   uk   *uk*

Snaky!

To make the second join, the pencil has to go from the baseline to the top of the ascender of the second letter. The join should be made in a smooth upward sweep of the hand.

These pairs of letters appear in common words such as *back* and *all*.

10

When you are using Join 2 to join to f or t, don't make it too spread out!

ch *ch*
sh *sh*
th *th*
il *il*
ll *ll*
ik *ik*
af *af*
ef *ef*
uf *uf*
ut *ut*

Ch, sh and th begin many common words (e.g. children, should, this). Regular practice will help with spelling as well as handwriting.

11

Try to make your writing flow!

Practise Join 2 in these school words.

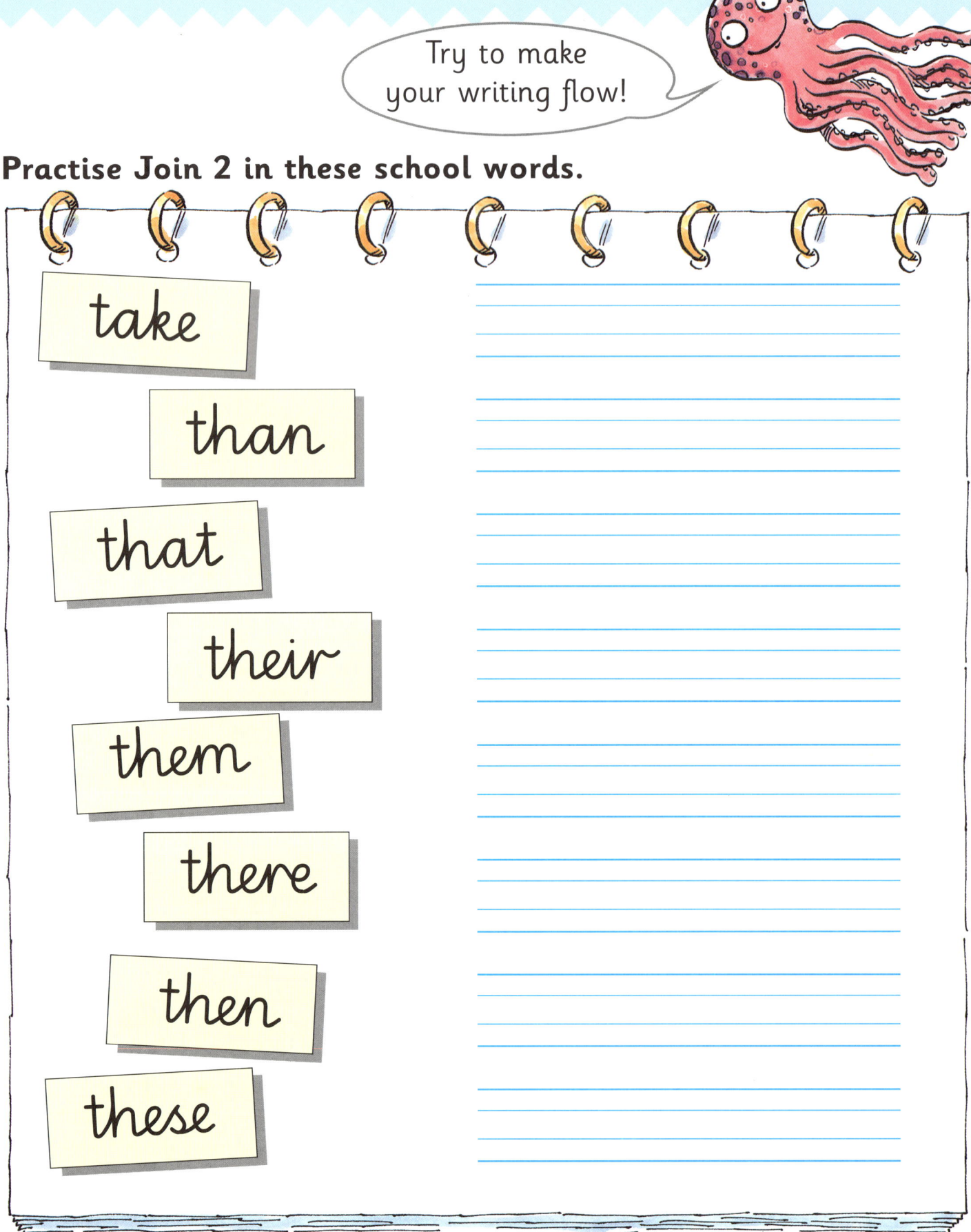

take

than

that

their

them

there

then

these

Practise Joins 1 and 2 when you are writing.

Practise Join 2 in these phrases.

pushing puss

pulling puss

many hands make it easy

The letter p is a breakaway letter (see page 22).

Let your child practise writing groups of words with the same spelling patterns (e.g. *kick, sick, click*). Make sure the words contain only the first and second joins at this stage.

Nice writing!

Join 3

Join 3
can join

Set 4
f o r v w

to

Set 2
a c d e g i j
m n o p q r s
u v w x y

oa

any letter in **Set 4**

any letter in **Set 2**

Practise Join 3.

oa oa   va va

wi wi   rd rd

og og   ro ro

The horizontal curve used to make the third join should not be too long. If it is, there will be too much space between the letters.

ov ov

or or

ox ox

os os

fa fa

ve ve

fe fe

wo wo

The letter e changes its shape according to which join comes before it.

Join 1 to e

me me

Join 3 to e

we we

Let your child practise making Join 1 and Join 3 to the letter e.

An octopus can change colour!

Practise Join 3 in these special colour names.

roasting red

deep dove

seaweed and sand

fiery sun

lemon cream

Look at a decorator's colour chart together. Encourage your child to make up some fanciful names for colours and to practise writing them. Draw guidelines like the ones in this book to help her.

Do I need this?

Practise Join 3 in these weather phrases.

chilly and snowy

wet and windy

sunny and warm

very misty

Ask your child to memorise a word before writing it. This will help her to write it in a single, fluid movement, without stopping to think about the spelling. If this is too difficult, she could memorise a couple of letters (e.g. *ch*, *ll*) at a time.

Well done! ⭐

Join 4

This is the last join!

Join 4
can join

Set 4
f o r
v w

any letter in **Set 4**

to

Set 3
b f h
k l t

any letter in **Set 3**

Practise Join 4.

ol ol

rh rh

oh oh

ob ob

ok ok

rk rk

rl rl

rb rb

Make sure that the diagonal stroke of the fourth join is
made at a tight angle. Children tend to spread it out too
much at first, leaving too much space between letters.
Give your child plenty of opportunities for practice.

wh : wh

fl fl

wl : wl

rk : rk

Take care
when you are joining
to f or t.

of

ot ōt

of ōf

rt : rt

rf : rf

ft ft

ff ff

Remember that your child should be sitting at a table when he writes. Make sure that the chair is high enough and that he is sitting fairly close to the table. This will help him to move his arm and hand freely.

He should rest the heel of his hand lightly on the page, and stretch his fingers to form the letters.

Practise Join 4 in these descriptions.
Match each description to the correct dog.

dark and fluffy

small and scowling

whiskery and willing

white and woolly

Keep a notebook in which your child can practise writing as neatly as possible. She will gain a sense of achievement from seeing her progress when she looks back through the book.

Practise Join 4 in these speech bubbles.

Point out that punctuation marks need to be written carefully.

Now that your child has learned all the joins, encourage her to practise by writing notes, cards and lists.

Excellent!

21

The breakaway letters

These eight letters are not followed by a join. They are called the **breakaway letters**.

The breakaway letters

b g j p
q x y z

No join is made to or from z.

lazy

Practise the breakaway letters in these words.

jam

yes

girl

boy

quilt

pot

axe

prize

A number of different handwriting schemes are used in schools; some of them teach children to join some of these eight letters. Check your child's school style before he starts this page, to avoid confusion.

Practise the breakaway letters in these descriptions of party food.

a great big yellow jelly

fizzy blue drinks

packets of crispy quivers

a mixture of green cakes

Remind your child to space letters and words evenly. Breakaway letters need to be spaced evenly, although they are not followed by a join.

Good work! ★

Writing capital letters

Copy each title on to one of the comics.

The title tells you what the comic is about.

KIDS' FUN   CRAZY CARTOONS

ZAPPO   AGENT X   ANIMALS FOR ME   ADVENTURE

KIDS'

Remind your child that all capital letters sit between the baseline and the top guideline.

Look for capital letters in newspapers, comics, advertisements and signs. Let your child make a nameplate for her bedroom door, with her name in capital letters.

Wonderful!

Writing a message

You have been shipwrecked on a desert island!
Send a message in a bottle.
Copy the message below.

Remember that a capital letter never joins to the next letter.

I am shipwrecked on a tropical island.

It is very hot and the jungle is noisy.

I have been here since August 1999.

Send ice lollies and a comic!

Best wishes from

Make sure your child signs the note!

Let her place a clear ruler or a narrow strip of paper under the line which is being copied, to mark the place.

Beautiful!

Jokes and rhymes

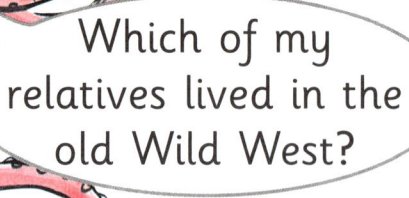

**Read the jokes and copy the punchlines.
Tell the jokes to someone.**

How can you tell which end of a worm is his head?

Answer
Billy the squid

Tickle his middle. Which end laughs?

_____
_____
_____

Which of my relatives lived in the old Wild West?

How does a sheep keep warm in winter?

By central bleating

_____
_____

What do you give a pony with a cold?

Cough stirrup

_____
_____

Why do bees have sticky hair?

Because they have honey combs

_____
_____

Children love jokes! To encourage more writing, let your child make a collection of favourite jokes in a notebook. Best handwriting should be used.

Funny rhymes like this one are called limericks.

Copy this rhyme.

There was a young ghost named Paul,
Who went to a fancy dress ball.
To surprise every guest,
He went there undressed,
But no one could see him at all!

(Anon)

Brilliant!

Writing a list

Copy Otis's list or write your own.

This is my wish list – a list of all the things an octopus would like!

Wish list

a clean ocean

no fishing nets

a dark cave

deep water

a soft sea bed

lots of babies

crabs to eat

If your child wants to write her own 'wish list', let her write it on a piece of paper first so that she can concentrate on what she wants to say. Correct the spelling if necessary, and then let her copy the list on to the page.

Fantastic!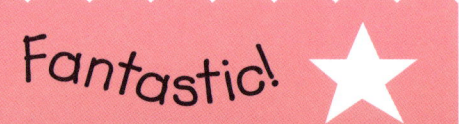

Writing a poem

Copy this poem.

Who?

Who?

Snoozing, snoring,

Then roaring at the

   postman.

Hair everywhere,

On Dad's chair!

Does he care?

Lying in the sun,

Going for a run,

Always fun,

My dog!

Read the poem together, looking for capital letters, breakaway letters and examples of each kind of join.

Encourage your child to concentrate on presentation when she copies the poem.

Well done! ★

29

Writing a story

Read this story opening.

I love sea tales!

It was a wild and windy night. The stars were bright in the dark sky. The clifftop road was empty. Suddenly there came a terrible noise. It was a …

Copy the story opening, or carry on with the story.

Encourage your child to memorise each
word before writing it, to aid fluency.

Excellent!

Filling in a form

This form is about a school trip.
Fill it in as if you were a parent or a carer.

Woodland Glade PRIMARY SCHOOL

Our school trip to Grimland Theme Park

Dear Parents,

This year we are going on a trip to somewhere really different!
The children will need to take wellingtons and a plastic bag.
Lunch is provided. Please fill in the form and return it quickly.

Yours sincerely,
Mrs. Fluffy (Head teacher)

Cost: £10.00 only

I give permission for my child:

to go to Grimland on 30th May. I enclose £10.00.

Return child at home time.

Signed

Did you remember
to sign the form?

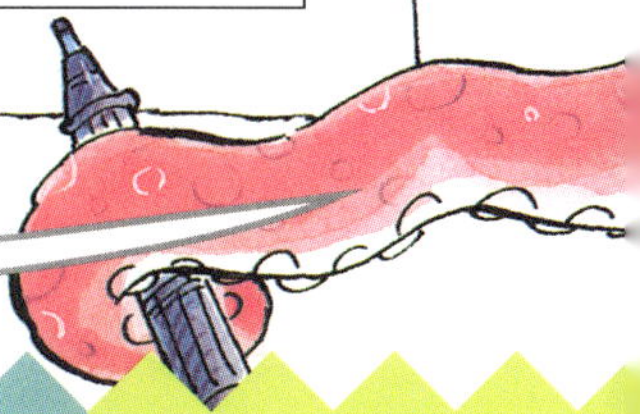

Your child should write his name in the space on the form, and then copy the three lines indicated.

Involve him when you are filling in forms, so that he is aware of this kind of functional writing.

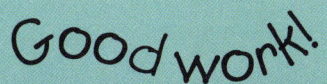

Good work! ★

31

See what I can do

Are you sitting comfortably?

I can write all these words in joined writing.

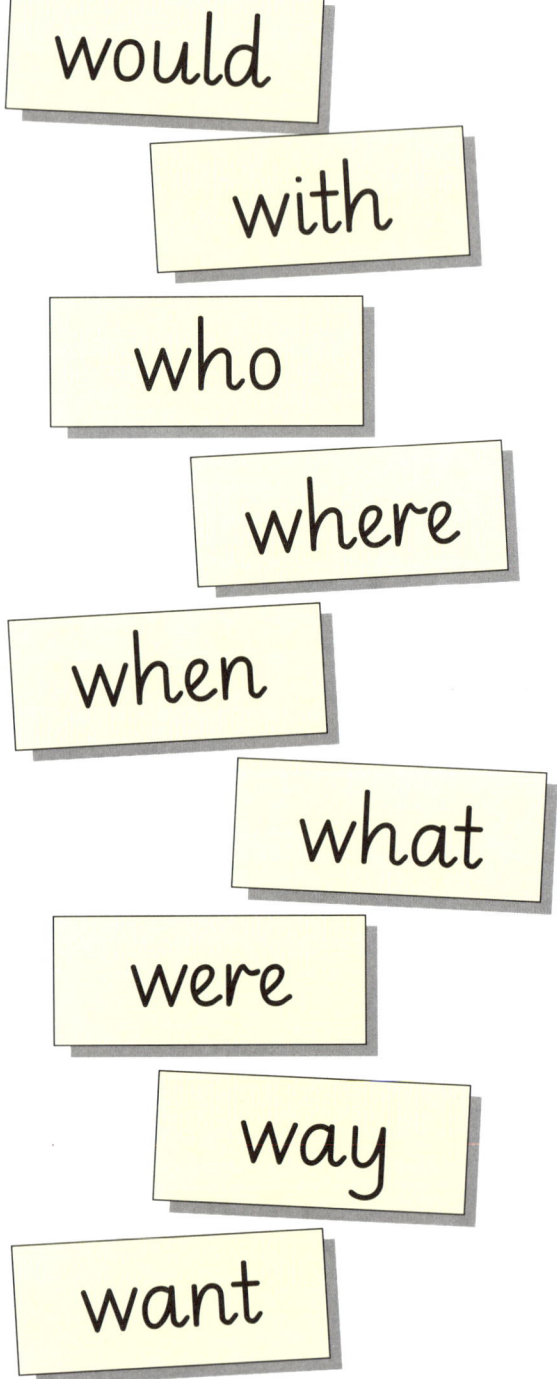

would

with

who

where

when

what

were

way

want

Ask your child to read each word and then to write it as neatly as possible. All the words are school words, and your child needs to be able to read and write them as they are very common.

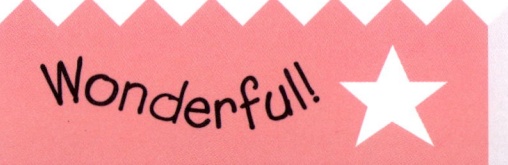

Wonderful!